Old Time String Band Music
for
MANDOLIN

BY JOSEPH WEIDLICH

ISBN 978-1-57424-302-4
SAN 683-8022

Cover by James Creative Group
Cover Photo: Bacon Mandolin, Artist model, 1921

Copyright © 2014 CENTERSTREAM Publishing, LLC
P.O. Box 17878 - Anaheim Hills, CA 92817

www.centerstream-usa.com

Table Of Contents
& CD Track List

Introduction 4

Basic Melodic Connections: A Traditional Approach 5

The Songs

A Dark Road is a Hard Road to Travel 12
A Message from Home Sweet Home 13
All Go Hungry Hash House [CD TRACKS 1-3] 15
All I've Got's Gone [CD TRACKS 4-5] 16
Are You Washed in the Blood? [CD TRACKS 6-7] 17
Careless Love 18
Don't Go Out Tonight, My Darling 18
Down on the Banks of the Ohio [CD TRACKS 8-9] 19
Fallen by the Wayside 19
Goodbye, Dear Old Stepstone [3/4 time] 21
Goodbye, Dear Old Stepstone [4/4 time] 22
Handsome Molly 23
He Is Coming After Me 24
He Is Coming to Us Dead 26
He Was Nailed to the Cross for Me 27
I Am Resolved 28
I Have Lost You Darling, True Love 29
I Know My Name Is There 29
I Remember Calvary 31
I Saw a Man at the Close of Day 32
I'll Never Be Yours 32
It's Sinful to Flirt 33
I've Always Been a Rambler 33
John Hardy [CD TRACKS 10-12] 34
Joke n' Henry 35
Little Maggie With a Dram Glass in Her Hand 36
Midnight on the Stormy Deep 36
Mountaineer's Courtship 37
My Mind is to Marry 37
My Mother and My Sweetheart 38
Never Be as Fast as I Have Been 40
New River Train 41
Nobody's Darling [CD TRACKS 13-14] 42
No More Goodbyes 43
On the Banks of Old Tennessee 44
Red or Green [The Red and Green Signal Lights] 45
Remember the Poor Tramp has to Live 46

Rose Conley 47
Sally Gooden 48
Say Darling Say 48
She's Mine, All Mine 49
Short Life of Trouble [CD TRACKS 15-16] 51
Shout Lula 51
Sweeping Through the Gates 52
Sweet Rosie O'Grady 52
The Burial of Wild Bill 53
The Eastbound Train 55
The Fate of Talmadge Osborne 56
The Lightning Express 57
The Nine Pound Hammer [CD TRACK 17-19] 59
The Nine Pound Hammer II 60
The Old Hickory Cane 61
The Old Maid and the Burglar 62
The Orphan Girl 63
The Pretty Mohea 64
The Prisoner's Lament 65
The Raging Sea, How It Roars 65
The Railroad Flagman's Sweetheart 66
The Religious Critic 66
The Resurrection 67
The Road to Washington [aka White House Blues]
[CD TRACKS 20-21] 68
The Titanic 68
The Wreck of the Southern Old 97 [CD TRACKS 22-23] 69
The Wreck on the C&O 70
There'll Come A Time 70
There's A Light Lit Up in Galilee 72
Too Late 72
Train No. 45 73
We Parted at the River 73
What You Gonna Do with the Baby 74
When the Redeemed are Gathering In 76
When the Snowflakes Fall Again 77
Where Are You Going, Alice? 77
You'll Never Miss Your Mother Until She's Gone

CD Track Aritst Index 78

Related Music Resources 78

Author's Biography 78

The Mandolin's Use in Old Time Music

Many of the songs recorded by string band artists in the 1920s and early 1930s were often rearrangements, in the truest folk tradition, of songs learned from a local community's oral tradition or perhaps "borrowed" from existing published song collections, child ballads, hymn books, etc., using new words and/or titles for a particular song. For instance, the melody for the song *The Battleship of Maine* was used for many other songs, including *White House Blues,* while the song *Sweet Sunny South* is found under the title *Take Me Home* in an 1882 banjo method with lyrics with an arranged banjo accompaniment; another example is that the melody for the song *Little Old Sod Shanty in the Lane* was reworked by Ernest V. Stoneman as *All Go Hungry Hash House.*

While many extant photos of string band artists show members holding a mandolin those instruments can barely be heard in most audio mixes on those recordings (even when cleaned up digitally), much less featuring a solo (fiddle or vocals reigned unless a jug band was being recorded, in which case a mandolin solo occasionally might be showcased). Therefore, this book provides you with an opportunity to learn over 70 Old Time Music (OTM) period songs that I transcribed as recorded mostly by Ernest Stoneman or the duo Grayson & Whitter during the 1920s and early 1930s. However, many of these songs were also covered by other string bands regardless of whether they had the opportunity to be commercially recorded or not.

The songs found in this collection were recorded, more-or-less, at relative concert pitch. For example, some artists such as Grayson & Whitter recorded many of their "sides" in the key of G while the key of D was a particular favorite of Ernest Stoneman; meanwhile, Charlie Poole recorded in a wide variety of keys. However, it was not unusual for performers to intentionally alter the tuning of their instruments to match their preferred vocal range, e.g., a half-step sharp or a half-step flat, or more.

A Note on the Transcription Process. As an example, when songs were performed in the key of B Flat Major I often transcribed them to the key of A Major, a half-step lower; likewise, if the song was in the key of F# Major I usually transcribed it one-half step higher, to G Major. The tonic key that I eventually chose for any one song was often easily confirmed by listening closely to the notes used in the alternating bass lines or walk-up lines used by the guitarists in their "seconding" backups as certain low notes are available in one chord family but not in another in certain tonic keys, thus dictating the preferred choice of key. Another contributing factor is that the equipment and/or media used for the recordings, either in the field or in recording studios, may not have been calibrated properly, e.g., they were recorded at more-or-less concert pitch during the recording process but accidentally altered during the transfer process, or vice versa.

In closing, what then are the elements of the old time mandolin style? To help answer that question in many instances I chose not to "smooth out" the melodic lines for a number of songs found in this collection as I thought it would be more valuable to include an additional variation or two in order for you to compare similar sections, thus learning how the melodic lines were altered harmonically or rhythmically by the artists. In this way you will begin to develop your own personal old time mandolin music style by attempting to imitate what those artists "laid down in wax." I have also included some related OTM music resources at the end of this book (if you can read music then *The Bickford Mandolin Method* [1920] will be particularly valuable).

Because staff notation is provided for all of these songs OTM fiddlers can also get in the act by simply adding their own personal bowing patterns, grace notes, etc., to them.

So, pick up your mandolin (or fiddle) and start having fun!

Joe Weidlich
Washington, DC

Basic Melodic Connections
A Traditional Approach

As you play through the songs in this collection you will come across certain types of note sequences more frequently than others. I would like to outline some of them for you here so that you can understand their function. This will allow you to "flesh out" the longer rhythmic lines found in vocal songs vs. traditional fiddle tunes, where these note sequences are visually more apparent due to the use of shorter note values. In fact, I decided not to "smooth out" many of the melodic lines in the songs presented here so that you can take the time to compare similar note passages and see how those lines are altered, either rhythmically or harmonically.

Turns. The function of the turn is to simply fill in space for a stationary note lasting for three quarter note beats. It usually consists of five eighth notes (lasting for the duration of three quarter note beats) in which the first, third and fifth notes are identical (in music theory terms this is called a *unison* note, i.e., notes sharing the same pitch), while the second and fourth notes are positioned immediately below or above the principal note (those notes are called, logically enough, *neighbor tones*).

Here is an example of the turn note sequence in G Major; in this instance the initial note is the Root of the G chord, G natural:

This 5-note figure can easily be reduced to a shuffle rhythm:

It is not unusual for the second eighth note not to be played, thus a short melodic variation results based on the root and its upper neighbor tone:

While the principal note of the turn is often the root of a chord, the third or the fifth of a chord can also be "turned."

There are several substitutions commonly used for the turn figure. These include a scale fragment called a *spin* (here based on the interval of a third) and *chord outlines*, which can be used to substitute for the spin itself.

The spin is a scale fragment that "spins away" from, then back to, the principal note, either descending or ascending (in this instance three beats):

Similarly, an ascending, descending or mixed chord outline can also be effectively used as a substitute because the first and last notes are the same:

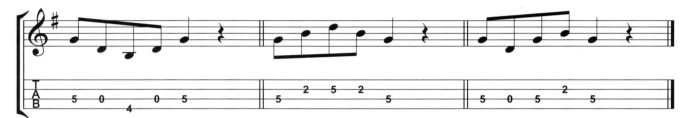

Now, let's compare the initial measure of two songs found in this collection where this technique is used: *A Dark Road is a Hard Road to Travel* and *Are You Washed in the Blood?*

A Dark Road ...   Are You Washed ...

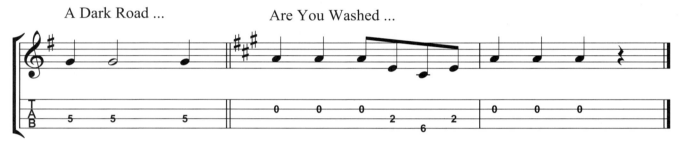

As you can see the first three beats in each song are based on the unison root note. In the second example a chord outline is used on beat three. Let's see how this note sequence works on the initial beat of the first example:

The lesson to be learned is to look at the melodic contour of the phrase to see what possibilities might exist in making variations, either melodically or rhythmically.

Now, let's move on and see how notes the interval of a third apart are connected. As you will, this note sequence is closely related to the turn and is used frequently.

Chord Tone Connectors. The basic difference between a turn and the chord tone connector is that the last note of the latter is positioned the interval of a third above or below the principal note.

Here is an example comparing a turn and an ascending chord tone connector based on the G chord:

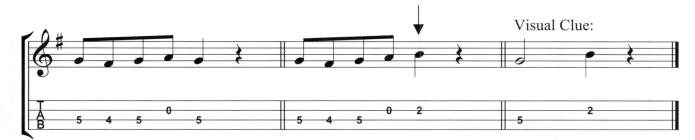

Since this note sequence connects adjacent chord tones the possibilities are from the Root to the third, the third to the fifth, and the sixth to the octave note.

Likewise, this connector phrase can be used in a descending motion, i.e., from the octave note down to the sixth, from the fifth down to the third, and from the third down to the root. Here is an example from the third to the root:

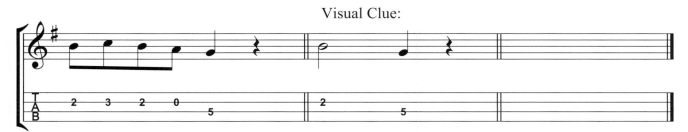

You should notice that the second note of the sequence moves in the opposite direction to the note of resolution, called *contrary motion*. In this way it creates a type of scale line that moves directly to the last note of the figure.

Chord tone connectors are used <u>to connect</u> adjacent chord tones; however, many substitutions can be employed for them. Let's first examine some ascending chord tone connector substitutions.

Similar to the turn, the second note of the sequence can simply be omitted:

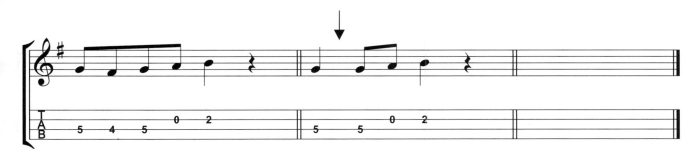

If the tempo is particularly fast you could even eliminate the passing tones as well:

Chord tones can also be effectively used as a substitute:

These same ideas can be used for descending chord tone connectors as well.

Now, let's look at measure five from the song *Careless Love* and see how we can use the ascending chord tone connector:

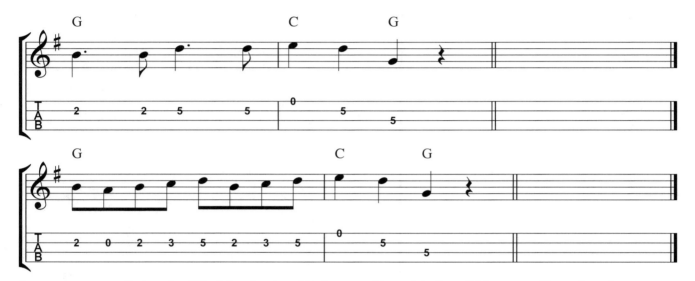

As you can see I simply filled in the implied ascending third to fifth ascending chord tone connector on beat one, then added a pick up scale line leading to the E note in the following measure (called a *3123 digital pattern*; more on those later on).

The 5-R Descending Scale Line. Next on the list is a descending scale line moving from the fifth of the scale (5) to its root (R). This note sequence is often used to approach the root at the end of a phrase:

This line is easily varied by use of an upper neighbor (scale) tone:

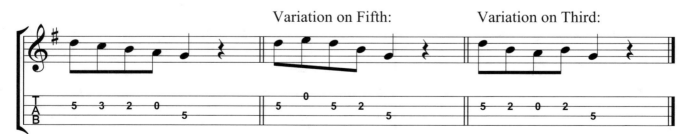

On occasion the sixth scale degree can be used as an upper neighbor on the downbeat to lead to the root:

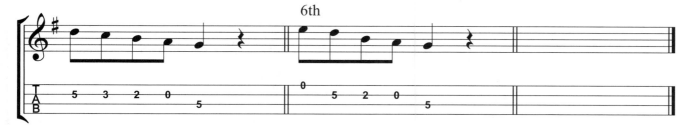

Now, let's look at measures 7-8 of the song *Don't Go Out Tonight, My Darling*:

As you can see on beat 3 of measure 7 the note D is the root of the D chord as well as the fifth of the G chord, thus you can use a descending 5-R Scale fragment here (see bracketed notes):

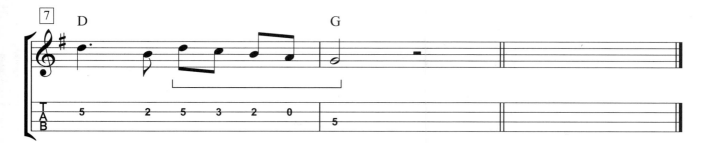

Did you notice that the first and third quarter notes in measure 7 are the same pitch, D? As this suggests a turn figure you might decide to play a chord outline or a spin (I chose a chord outline here):

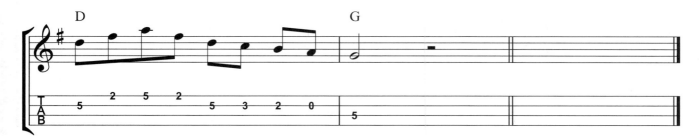

In fact, you could just as easily use two descending chord tone connectors:

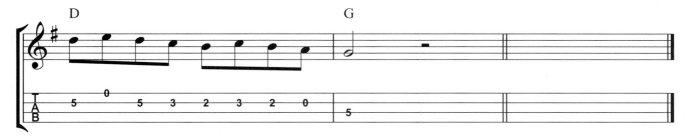

As you can see, once you get used to seeing when to use these type of note sequences opportunities easily open up to you.

The 1235 Digital Scale Pattern. Now, let's look at an ascending scale pattern that I abbreviate as **1235**, that is the first, second, third and fifth notes of a scale:

This note sequence is frequently used to outline a triad. Occasionally, the second note may be missing, particularly at phrase endings, so you can fill it in to create some rhythmic forward motion:

Here is how it might be used in the song *New River Train* (measure 6):

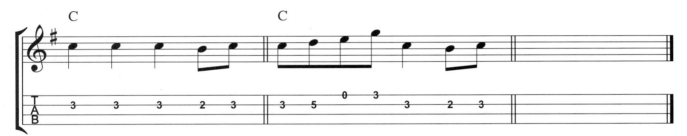

Since the first and third notes are the same here, this note sequence could also be used as a variation on a turn figure.

This digital pattern is also useful in a V-I chord change where the "1" is the root of the V chord. As a result, the last note of the pattern is the supertonic of the G major scale that resolves downward by a whole step:

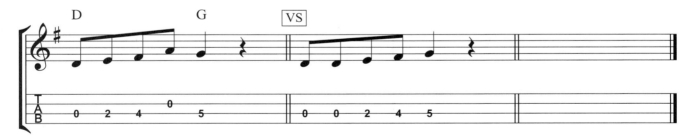

Other Useful Digital Patterns. To finish up I want to discuss some other commonly used four-note digital patterns where the first and last notes are the same (the "x"s in measure 3 indicate where the notes go up or down the scale):

Here are the four basic scale fragment patterns:

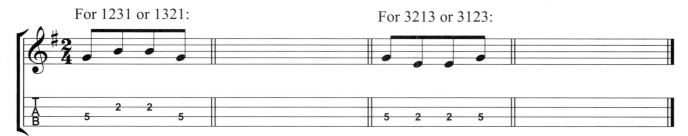

These patterns are often played this way (particularly in fiddle tunes):

Let's look at an example where this altered pattern can be used, here in the first measure of *John Hardy*:

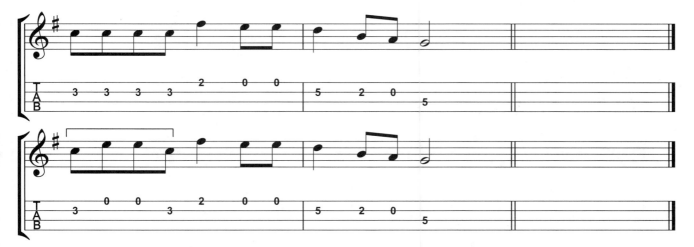

Did you also notice the abbreviated descending 5-R scale leading to G in the last measure?

Summing up, I hope that the examples which I have provided above offer you a useful tool to help you to become aware of some of the many ways that melodic lines in phrases can be reshaped and how you can often use "traditional" note sequences to substitute for them. Let the melodic contour be one of the guides in helping you create your own personal interpretations of these classic string band songs!

A Dark Road Is A Hard Road to Travel

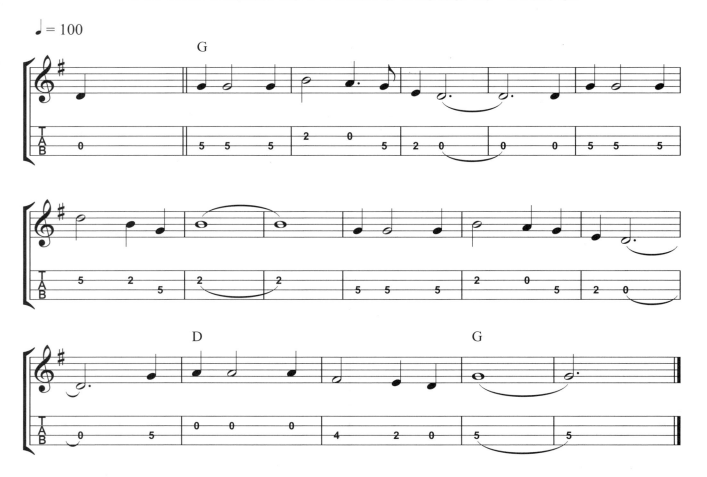

A Message From Home Sweet Home

All Go Hungry Hash House

♩ = 98

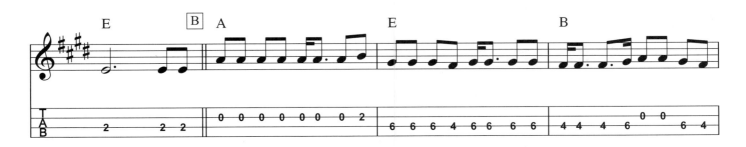

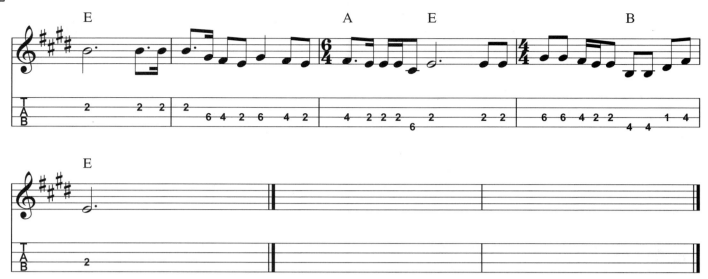

All I've Got's Gone

Are You Washed In The Blood?

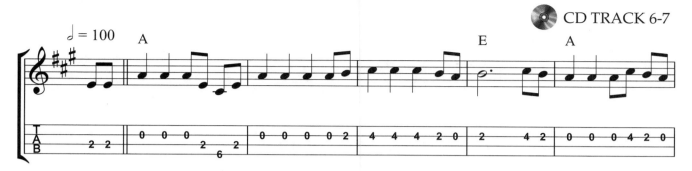

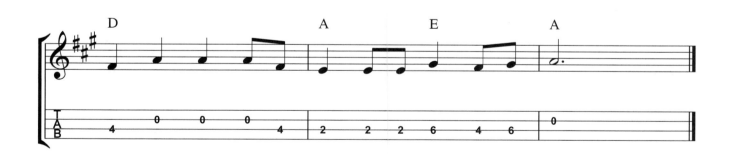

Careless Love

Don't Go Out Tonight, My Darling

Down on the Banks of the Ohio

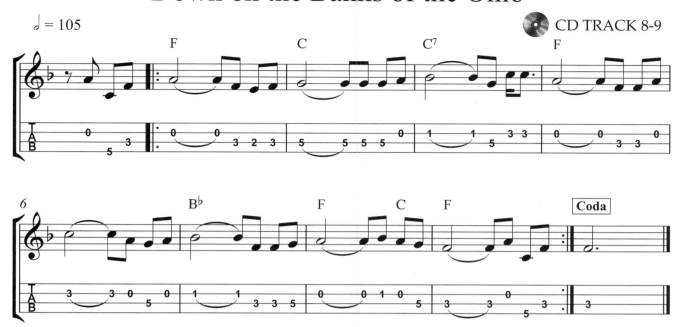

Fallen By The Wayside

Goodbye, Dear Old Stepstone

Goodbye Dear Old Stepstone

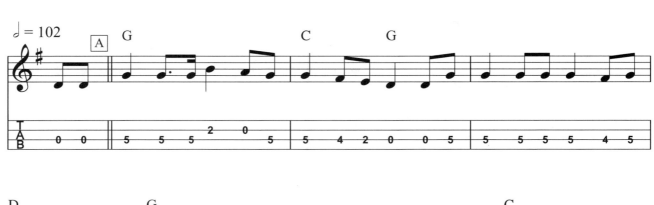

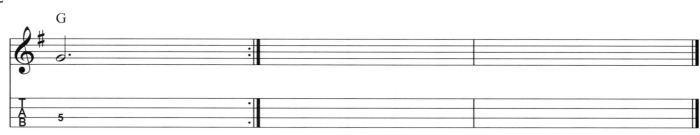

Handsome Molly

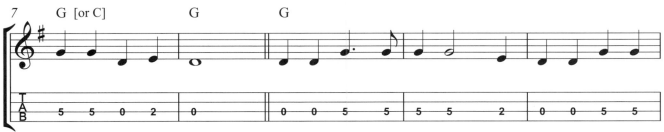

He Is Coming After Me

♩ = 100

2

Young guitarist Ernest V. Stoneman and his Dixie Mountaineers from Galax Virginia

He Is Coming To Us Dead

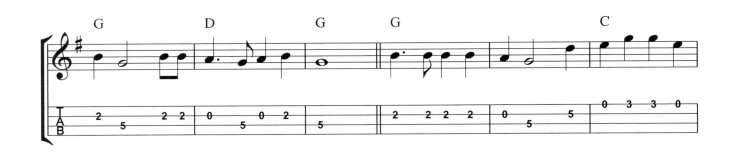

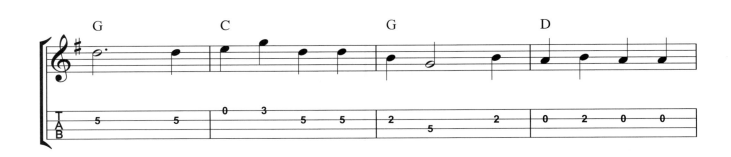

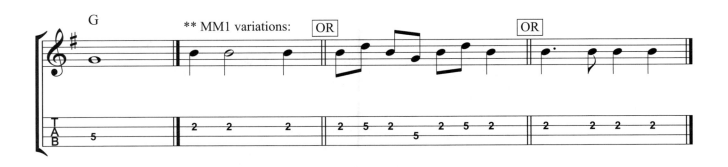

He Was Nailed To The Cross For Me

I Am Resolved

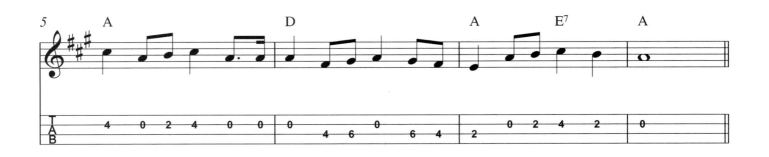

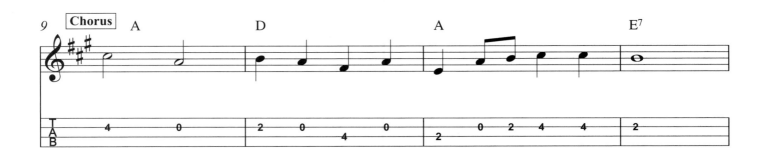

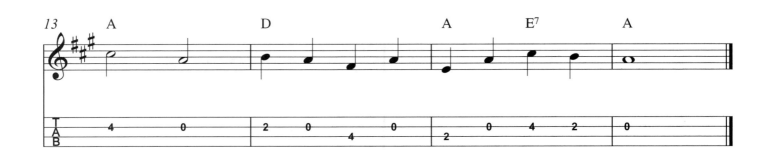

I Have Lost You Darling, True Love

I Know My Name Is There

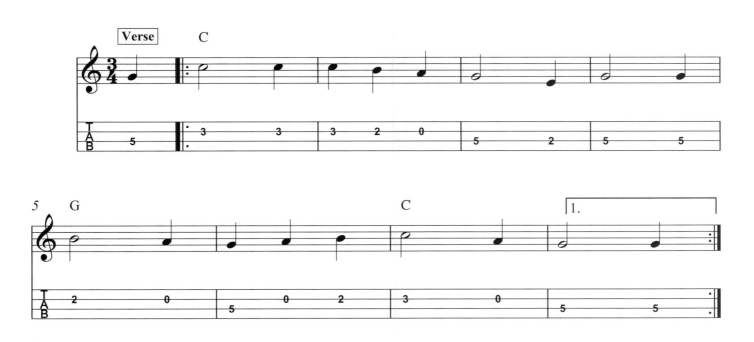

I Remember Calvary

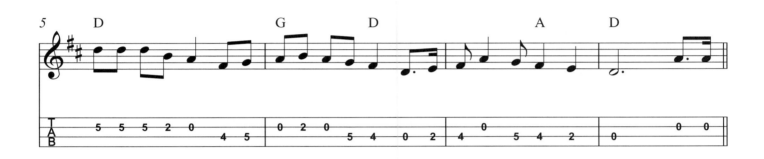

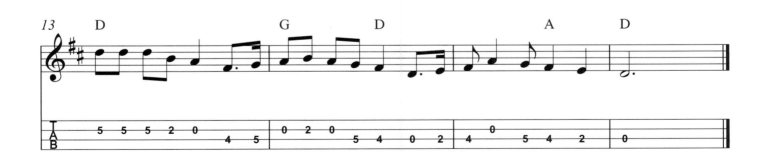

I Saw A Man at the Close of Day

I'll Never Be Yours

It's Sinful To Flirt

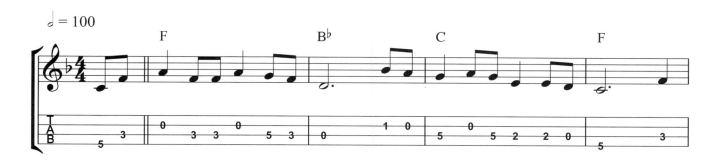

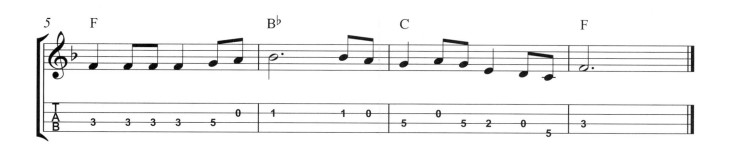

I've Always Been A Rambler

John Hardy

CD TRACK 10-12

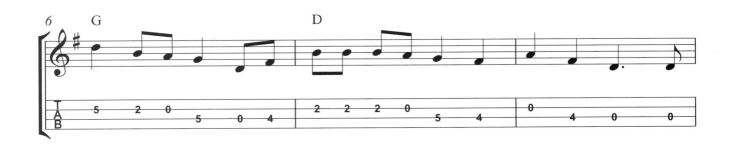

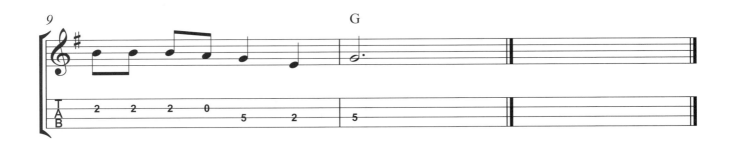

34

Joke 'n Henry

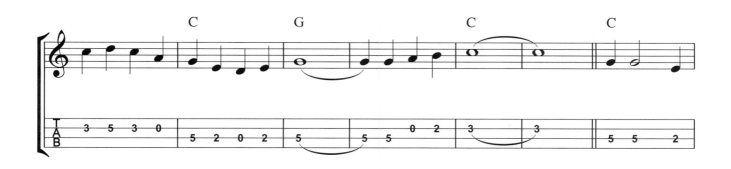

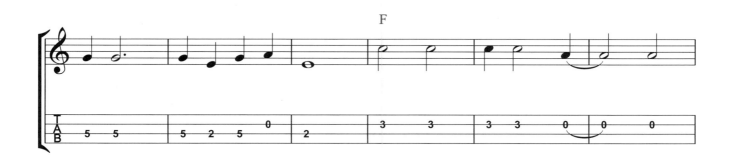

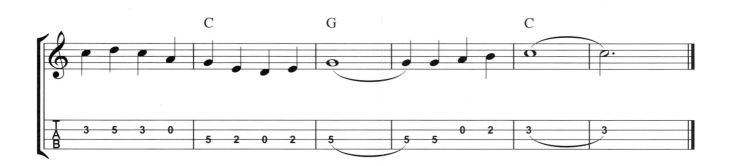

Little Maggie With a Dram Glass in Her Hand

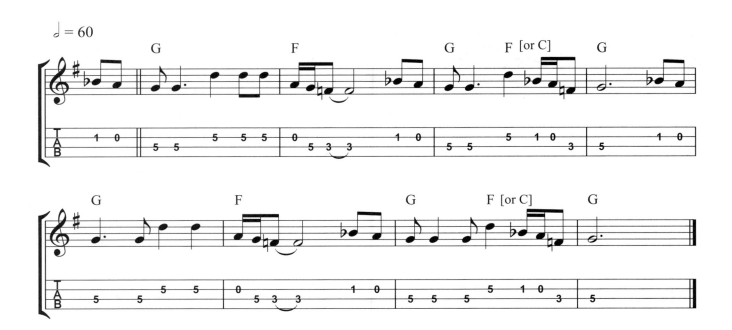

Midnight on the Stormy Deep

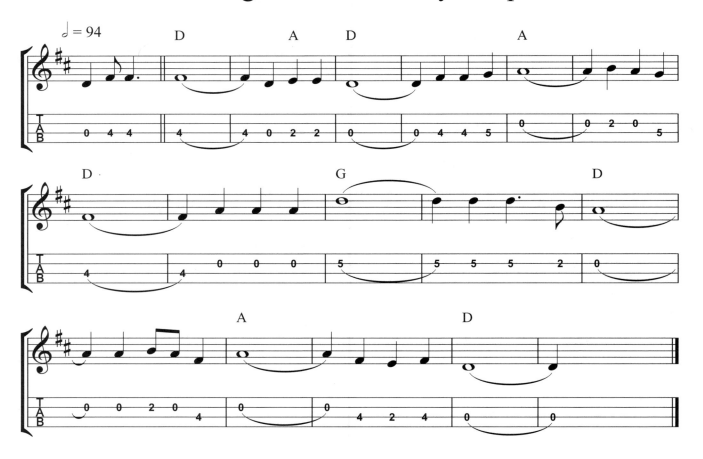

Mountaineer's Courtship

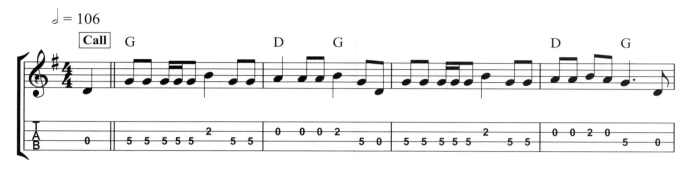

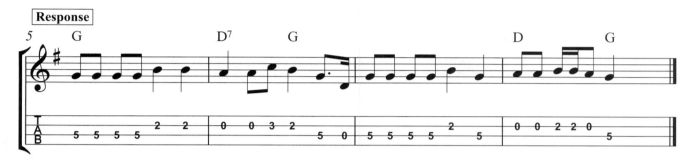

My Mind Is To Marry

My Mother and My Sweetheart

2

Never Be As Fast As I Have Been

New River Train

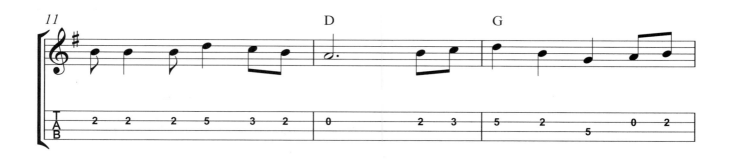

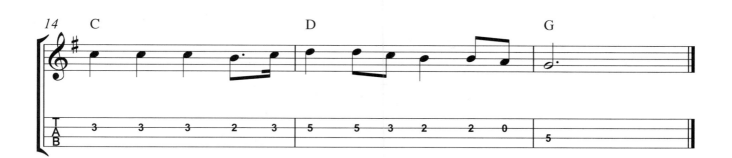

Nobody's Darling

No More Goodbyes

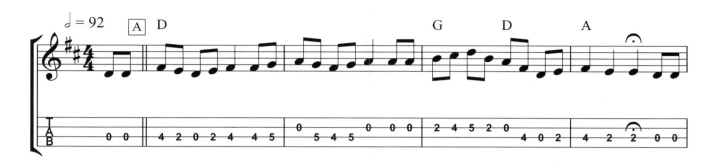

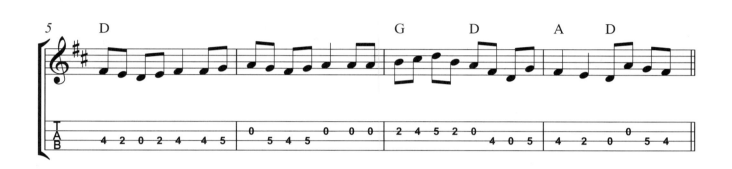

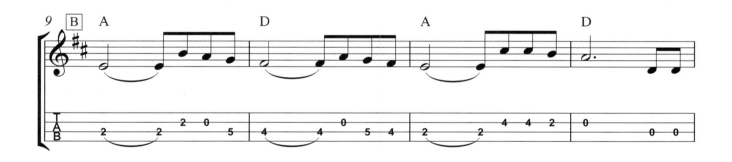

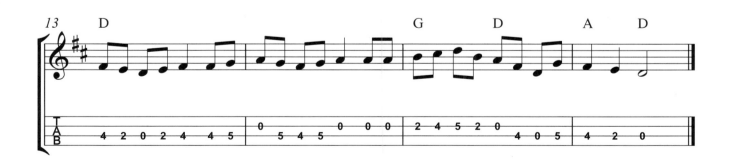

On the Banks of Old Tennessee

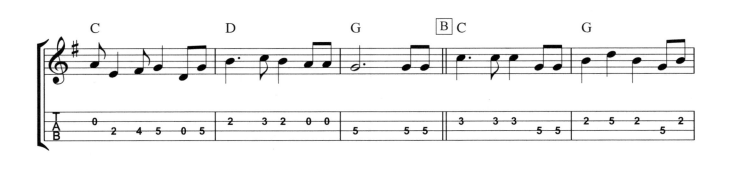

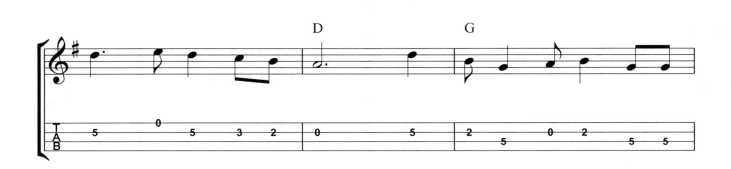

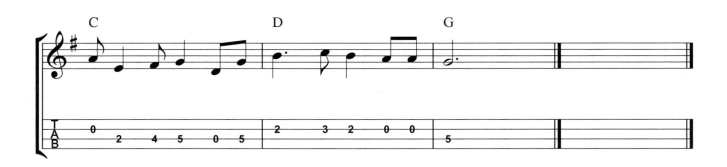

Red or Green
aka The Red and Green Signal Lights

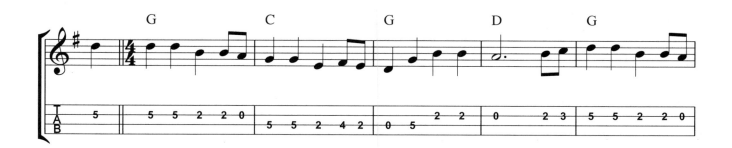

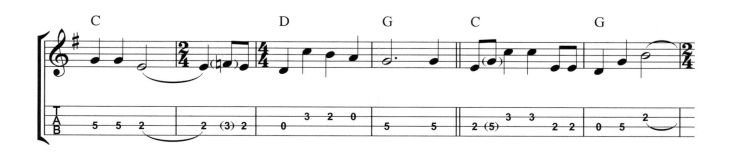

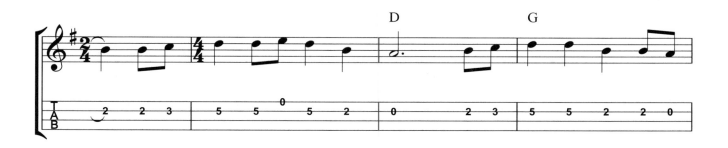

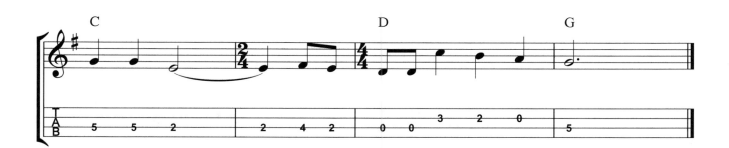

Remember the Poor Tramp Has to Live

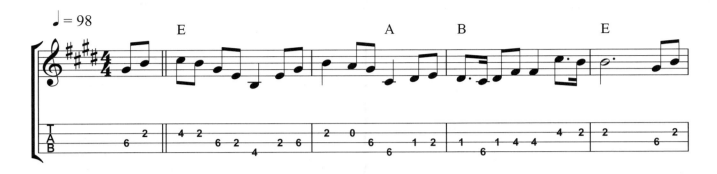

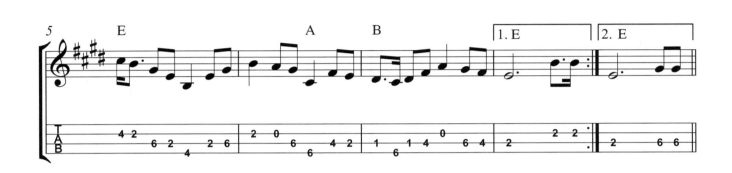

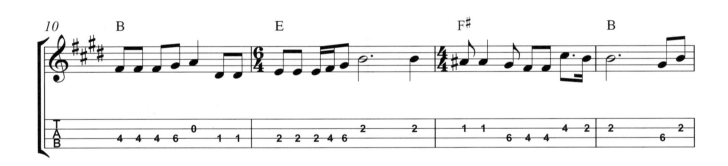

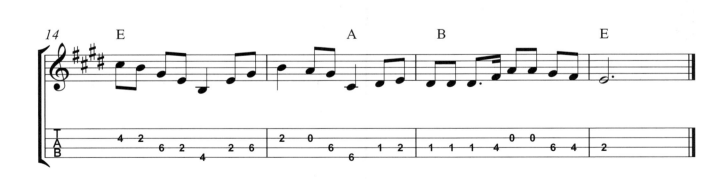

Rose Conley

♩. = 60

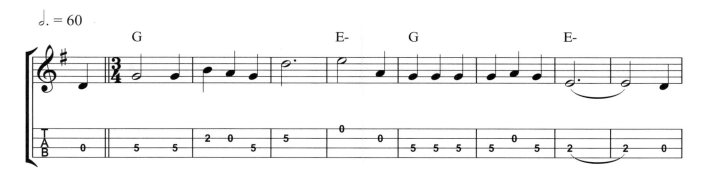

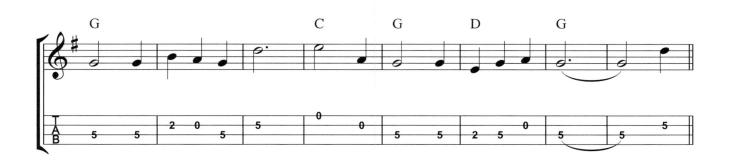

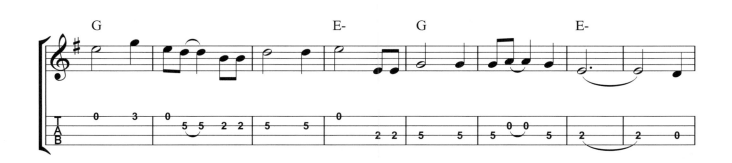

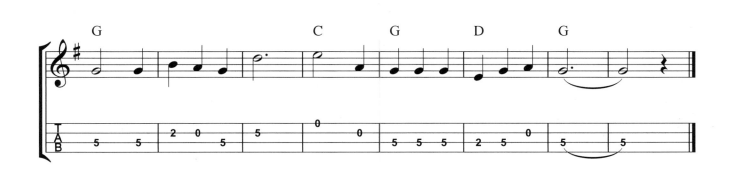

Sally Gooden

Play over vocal

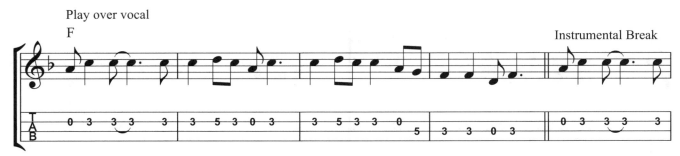

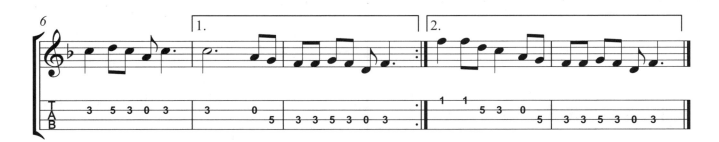

Say Darling Say

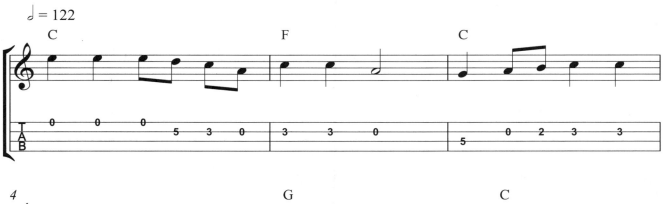

She's Mine, All Mine

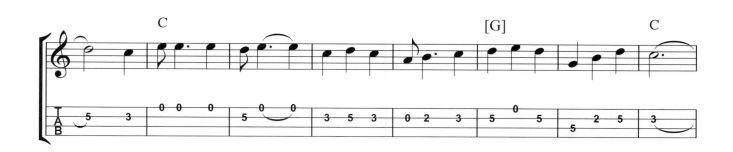

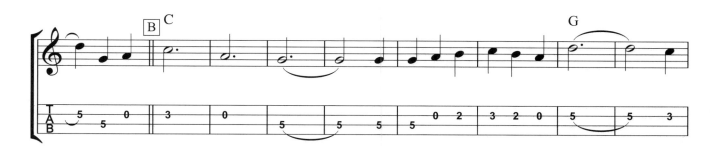

2

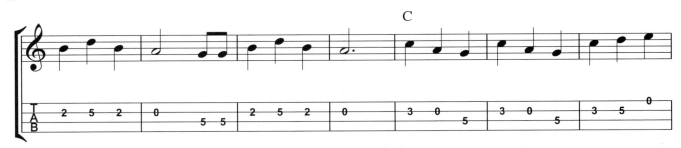

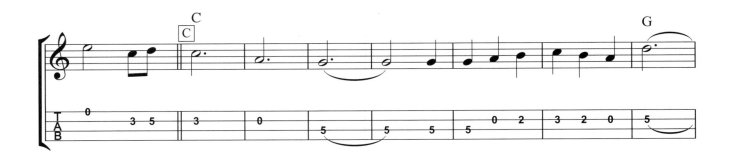

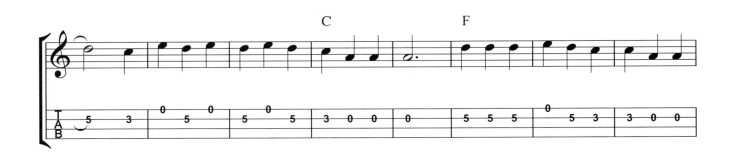

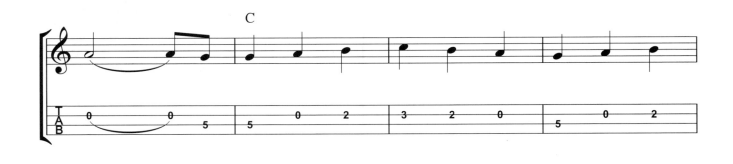

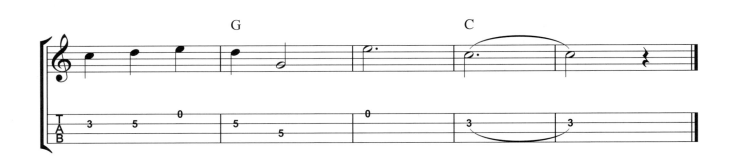

Short Life Of Trouble

CD TRACK 15-16

Shout Lula

Sweeping Through The Gates

Sweet Rosie O'Grady

The Burial of Wild Bill

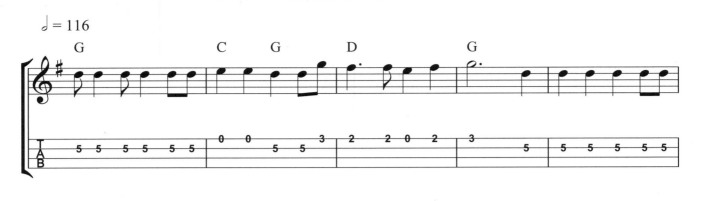

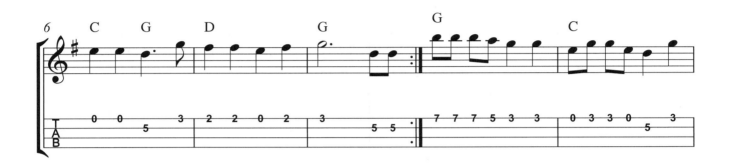

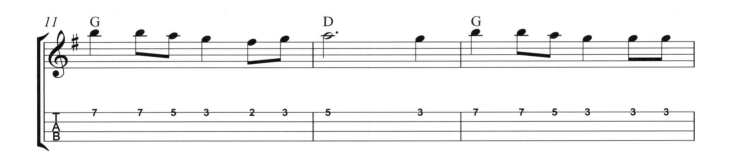

The Eastbound Train

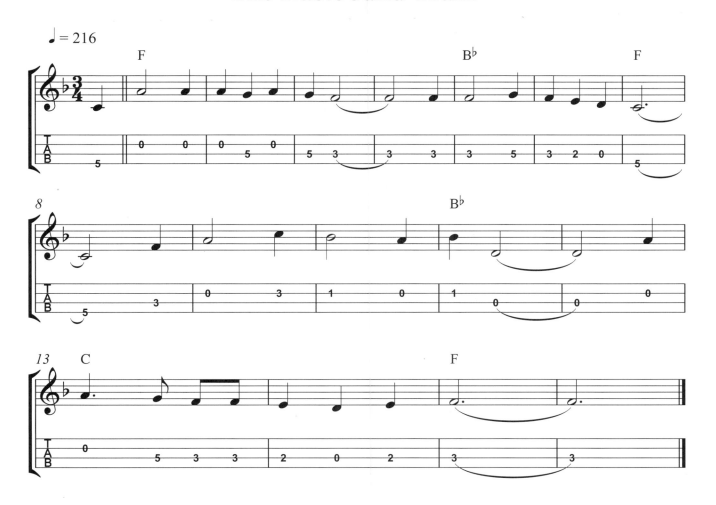

The Fate of Talmadge Osborne

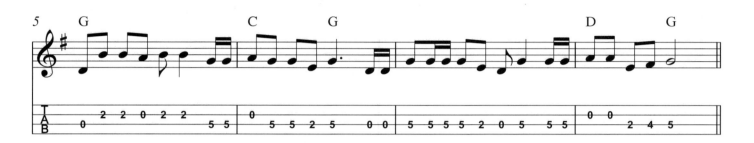

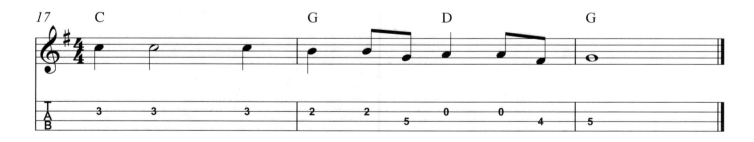

The Lightning Express

The Nine-Pound Hammer

 CD TRACK 17-19

The Nine Pound Hammer

♩ = 100

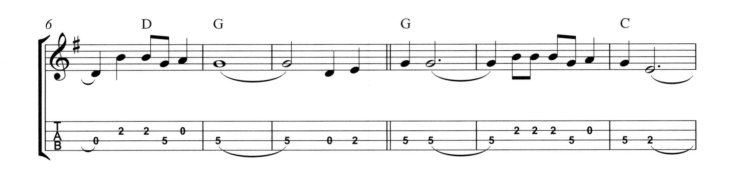

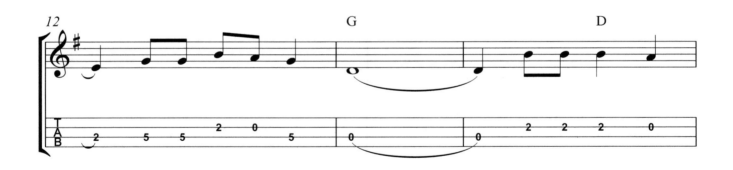

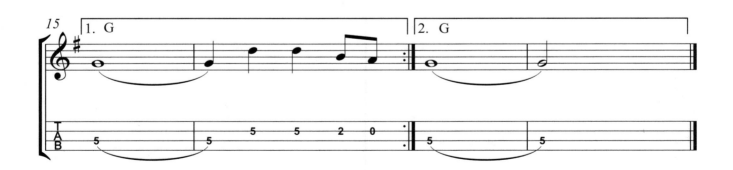

The Old Hickory Cane

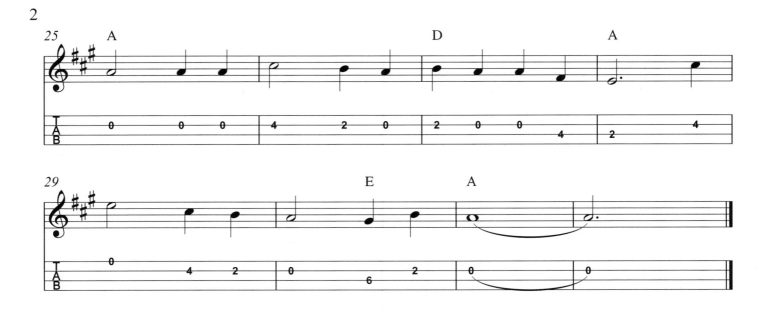

The Old Maid and the Burglar

The Orphan Girl

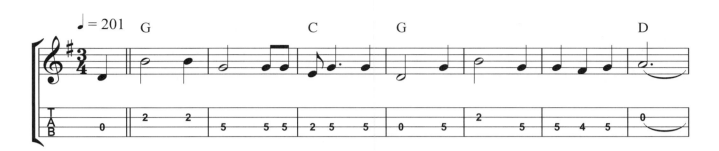

The Pretty Mohea

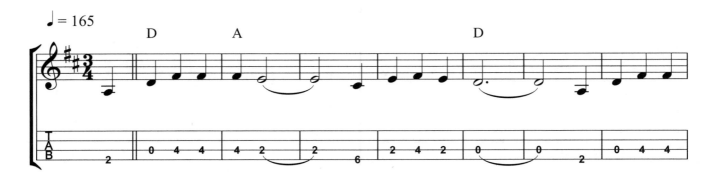

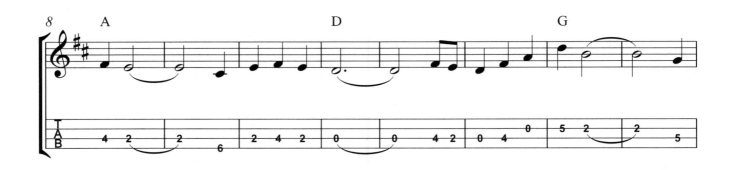

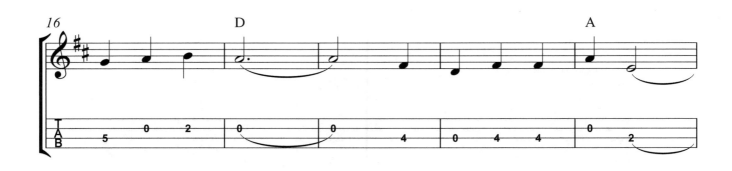

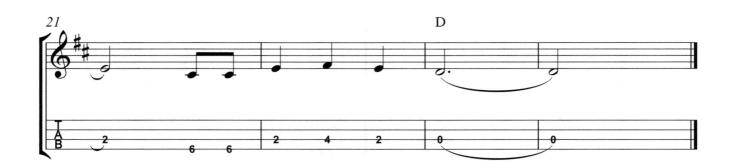

The Prisoner's Lament

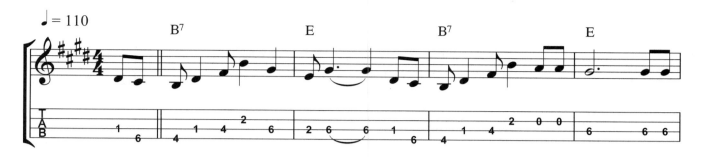

The Raging Sea, How It Roards

The Railroad Flagman's Sweetheart

The Religious Critic

The Resurrection

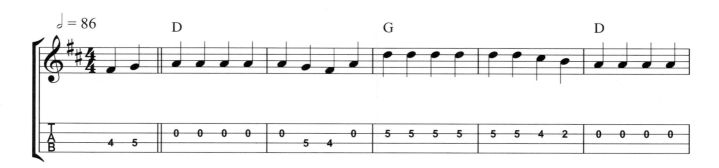

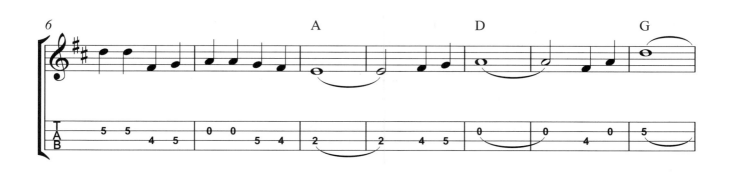

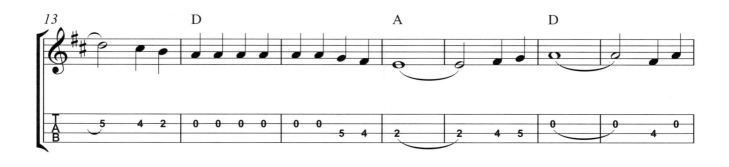

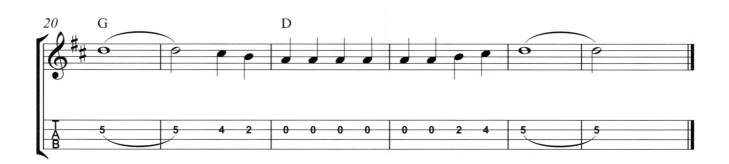

The Road to Washington
aka White House Blues

The Titanic

68

The Wreck of the Southern Old 97

CD TRACK 22-23

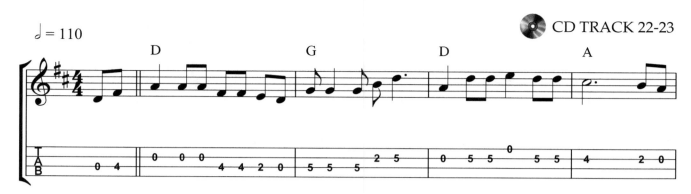

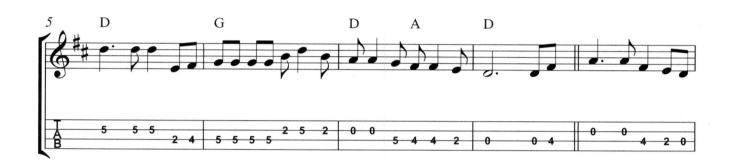

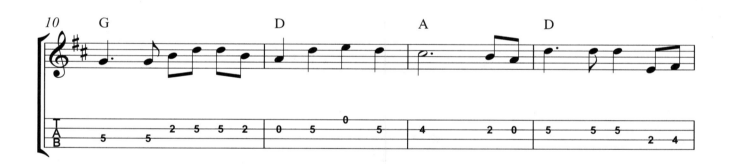

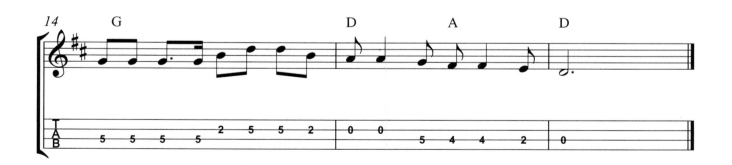

The Wreck on the C&O

There'll Come A Time

There's A Light Up In Galilee

Too Late

Train No. 45

We Parted at the River

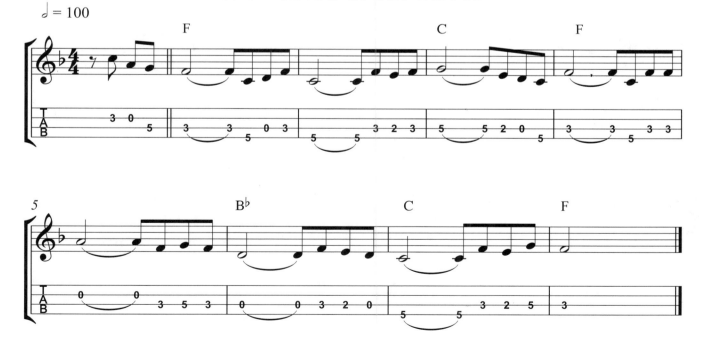

What You Gonna Do With The Baby

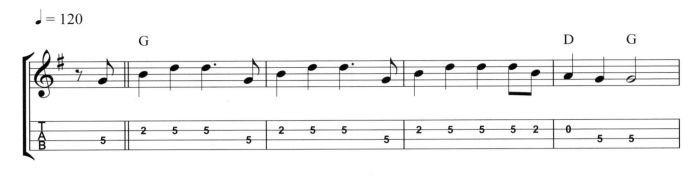

When the Redeemed Are Gathering In

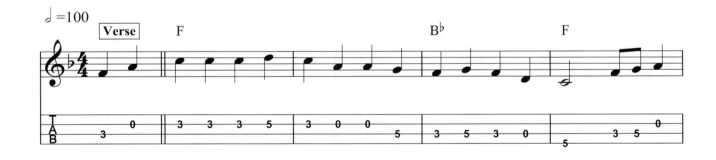

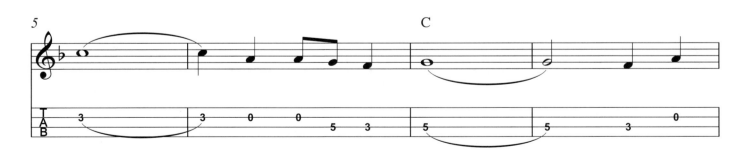

When the Snowflakes Fall Again

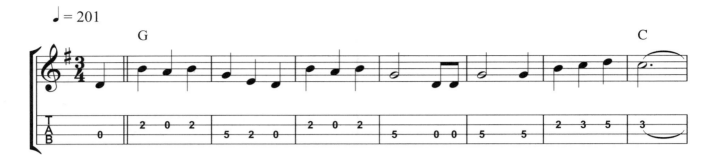

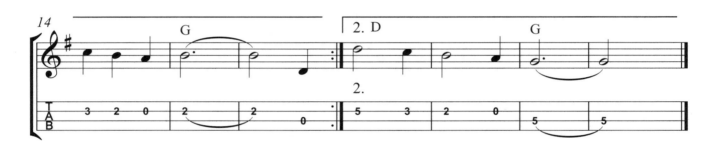

Where Are You Going Alice?

You'll Never Miss Your Mother Until She's Gone

CD Track Artist Index

All Go Hungry Hash House. Track 1: Ernest Stoneman, 2: Charlie Poole, 3: Uncle Dave Macon [Page 15]

All I've Got's Gone. Track 4: Ernest Stoneman, 5: Uncle Dave Macon [Page 16]

Are You Washed in the Blood? Track 6: Ernest Stoneman, 7: Da Costa Woltz [Page 17]

Down on the Banks of the Ohio. Track 8: Ernest Stoneman, 9: Grayson & Whitter [Page 19]

John Hardy. Track 10: Buell Kazee, 11: Walter Williams, 12: Ernest Stoneman [Page 34]

Nobody's Darling. Track 13: North Carolina Ridge Runners, 14: Grayson & Whitter [Page 42]

Short Life of Trouble. Track: 15, Grayson & Whitter, 16: Burell Kazee [Page 51]

The Nine Pound Hammer. Track 17: Frank Blevins & His High Tar Heel Rattlers, 18: Grayson & Whitter, 19: Ernest Stoneman. [Page 59]

The Road to Washington. Track 20: Ernest Stoneman, 21: Charlie Plloe [Page 68]

The Wreck of the Southern Old 97. Track 22: Henry Whitter, 23: Ernest Stoneman [Page 69]

Related Music Resources

Old Time Mandolin Music Website [www.oldtimemandolinmusic.com]

The Bickford Mandolin Method by Zarh Myron Bickford (1920), published by Carl Fisher (NY); also available as an e-book from www.DjangoMusic.com

Old Time Country Music (for mandolin) by Mike Seeger

Mandolin for Dummies® by Don Julin

Chapter 9 discusses the old time music genre.

The Mandolin of Norman Blake: Traditional and Original Tunes and Techniques [DVD]

The Mandolin Picker's Guide to Bluegrass Improvisation by Jesper Rübner-Petersen. See Chapters 17-19 on basic double stop usage.

Old Time Mandolin Tunes & Tips by Carl Jones [DVD]

String Band Classics of The Fuzzy Mountain String Band, arranged for mandolin by Dix Bruce

Author's Biography

Joseph Weidlich began his formal musical studies on the classic guitar, moving to Washington, D.C. from his native St. Louis to teach that instrument. He published a series of renaissance lute transcriptions for classic guitar which were distributed by G. Schirmer. In the early music genre he has played renaissance guitar, renaissance lute and baroque guitar.

Over the last 15 years Weidlich has written a number of books on 1920s-early 1930s string band music, early country guitar backup styles, Swing Era jazz guitar, and antebellum banjo styles. Reviews of his books have appeared in Acoustic Guitar magazine, the Old Time Herald, Banjo Newsletter, the Ozark Mountaineer and Dirty Linen. Weidlich has also written articles which have appeared in music journals and newsletters which have subsequently been cited as source material in related research and early music doctoral dissertations including *Battuto Performance Practice in Early Italian Guitar Music* (1606-1637) for the Journal of the Lute Society of America (Volume XI) which outlined the various strumming practices found in early guitar methods published in Italy and Spain in the early 17th century.

More Great Mandolin Books from Centerstream...

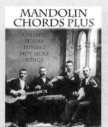

MANDOLIN CHORDS PLUS

by Ron Middlebrook

Features chords, scales, tunings, hot licks and songs. Shows over 300 chord fingerings, 18 hot licks used for intros, endings and turn-arounds, how to read tablature, several scales and 2 songs..

00000040 ....$3.75

MANDOLIN CHRISTMAS

arr. Eric Cutshall

18 favorites, each presented in two versions: a simple lead sheet arrangment with melody, lyrics and chords; and an advanced solo arrangement that combines the melody and accompaniment. Includes: Adeste Fideles • Deck the Halls • The First Noel • Good King Wenceslas • Jingle Bells • and more.

00001209 Softcover...9.95

ASAP BLUEGRASS MANDOLIN

Learn How to Play the Bluegrass Way
by Eddie Collins

This book/2-CD pack delivers the meat and potatoes of bluegrass mandolin way beyond just teaching fiddle tunes! Players will discover how to find their way around the neck using common double stops, develop creative back-up skills, play solos to vocal tunes in the style of Bill Monroe, make up their own solos, and a whole lot more. For the average learner, this pack represents nearly two years worth of lessons! Includes two (2) instructional CDs: one plays every example in the book, and the 2nd contains 32 songs performed by a bluegrass band with the mandolin parts separated on the right channel.

00001219 Book/2-CD Pack $24.95

ASAP IRISH MANDOLIN
by Doc Rossi

Doc Rossi, a well-known musician in both traditional and early music, has created this book for mandolin players who want to improve their technique, develop ideas and learn new repertoire ASAP.

The tunes in this book have been arranged by genre and in order of difficulty. Starting with the basics of ornamentation in traditional Irish music, Doc then goes directly into the tunes, in tablature and standard notation. Right-hand and left-hand techniques, ornamentation and other topics are taught through the tunes themselves.

00128349 Book/CD Pack $19.99

OLD TIME STRING BAND MUSIC FOR MANDOLIN

by Joe Weidlich

70 Old Time Music Period Songs. Many of the songs recorded by string band artists in the 1920s and early 1930s were often rearrangements, in the truest folk tradition, of songs learned from a local community's oral tradition or "borrowed" from existing published song collections, child ballads, hymn books, historical events, etc., using new words and/or titles for a particular song. Pick up your mandolin and start having fun!

00128131 Book/CD Pack $19.99

P.O. Box 17878 - Anaheim Hills, CA 92817
(714) 779-9390   www.centerstream-usa.com

More Great Guitar Books from Centerstream...

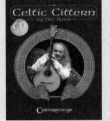
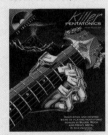

P.O. Box 17878 - Anaheim Hills, CA 92817
(714) 779-9390   www.centerstream-usa.com